KT-134-5

Delivering the Promise
Making e-learning strategy work

Bob Powell

Published by the National Institute of Adult Continuing Education
(England and Wales)

21 De Montfort Street
Leicester LE1 7GE
Company registration no. 2603322
Charity registration no. 1002775

Copyright © 2009 National Institute of Adult Continuing Education

(England and Wales)

All rights reserved. No reproduction, copy or transmission of this publication
may be made without the written permission of the publishers, save in
accordance with the provisions of the Copyright, Designs and Patents Act 1988,
or under the terms of any licence permitting limited copying issued by the
Copyright Licensing Agency.

promoting adult learning

NIACE, the national organisation for adult learning, has a broad remit to
promote lifelong learning opportunities for adults. NIACE works to develop
aresources.

NIACE's website www.niace.org.uk

Cataloguing in Publication Data
A CIP record of this title is available from the British Library

ISBN
978 1 86201 382 7

Typeset and designed by Creative by Design, Paisley
Printed by Page Bros, Norwich

Contents

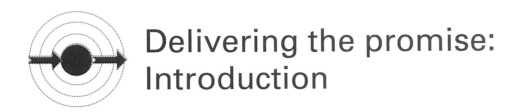

Delivering the promise: Introduction

This publication aims to help you to put your information and communications technology (ICT)/e-learning strategy into practice – to make it work in the real world. It does this by building upon the experiences that a number of Adult and Community Learning (ACL) organisations have had with their e-learning strategies as part of NIACE's e-learning strategy work. The target audience is leaders and those who want to lead. In the field of e-learning, leadership can be found on just about every rung of the management ladder.

E-learning strategy

Successive government initiatives have encouraged institutions in post-16 education to have a strategy for e-learning. NIACE published guidelines for putting together such a strategy in ACL in 2002 as part of the National Learning Network (NLN) initiative. These asked large services to develop a written strategy covering the following issues:

1. Vision for e-learning
2. The national, regional and local strategic framework
3. Management of the strategy
4. Infrastructure for e-learning
5. Teaching and learning practice
6. Staff development
7. Content and materials
8. Support services

Smaller providers were encouraged to undertake a less demanding process built upon answering questions about what they would like to do with regard to e-learning and the implications of their intentions for staff, learners, finance and resources.

The process of developing an e-learning strategy starts with a vision for the contribution that you wish it to make to learning and teaching in the institution and what you need to put in place to achieve this. The strategy needs a time-scheduled action plan, together with a budget to turn it from a wish list into reality.

In general, strategies and action plans are over-optimistic. Success seems to take longer than expected and achieve less than leaders hoped. Case studies and reports seem to gloss over the reality and put a good face on it. Despite this, many organisations do manage to deliver the main strands of their strategy successfully and there is evidence that education is changing – and has indeed changed – as a result.

If you were not involved in putting your institution's strategy together, then now would be a good time to get hold of a copy and consider how far you think it applies – and has been applied – in practice before reading on.

From strategy to practice

There is no single right way to put strategy into practice, nor any trouble-free guaranteed route, but a structured approach is likely to be more successful than a series of well-meaning, but essentially haphazard activities. The approach suggested here is built around a simple four-stage sequential model of activity that identifies where you need to start and where you go from there. It is based upon the idea that in order to achieve your aims you must:

- know what you want to do
- get the key resources in place to enable you to do it
- communicate your intentions to staff and other stakeholders
- train, prepare and resource them to do it
- motivate and support their further development
- monitor, review and revise in the light of experience.

Three assertions underpin the model, with important implications for putting e-learning strategy into practice.

1. The purpose of educational establishments is to deliver learning

Education seeks to bring together purposeful and effective teaching with productive learning activity. The key measure of impact at the end of each cycle of your strategy, therefore, is not how many computers you have or how many staff have attended training programmes, but whether and to what extent teaching and learning practice has changed for the better. Measures of computer stock, staff development, content and so on constitute important milestones, to be monitored, reviewed and actively managed, but the end goal is to improve and enrich practice.

2. Management is about getting other people to do things

Since the principal focus of e-learning strategy is to change teaching and learning practice, this self-evidently means getting teachers, their line managers and learners to do things differently. Before this can happen, managers have to build the capacity and capability to change practice: put infrastructure in place, train staff and get hold of suitable resources, advice and guidance. The first job for managers is the often difficult one of getting the money to spend on these things. Successive rounds of government support have provided generous pump-priming funding in all sectors of education. The pressure to spend these sums before budget year end, however, has often meant that management teams have been forced to decide their strategies earlier and more quickly than they would prefer.

The drive has been to answer the question

- *What do we want to buy?*

before they have answers to questions such as:

- *What do we want to happen in the classroom or workshop?*
- *What do we want staff and other stakeholders to do?*

Organisations invest in infrastructure and other strategic assets in order to implement their strategy. These are enabling investments. They make it possible for staff to change their practice. They include tangible assets such as a learning platform and online content and intangibles such as the development of in-house expertise that comes from training staff and the time required for skills development. These strategic assets make it **possible** for teaching and learning to change. Practice will only change if practitioners are able to make effective use of them.

3. Teachers want to do their job well

Tutors want to do their best for learners. This can lead those who are already doing a good job to be sceptical about innovation and to a heightened sense of the risks involved in changing practice. The aim of the strategy is to change the practice of teachers and learners, which means that managers must ensure that tutors understand the benefits and challenges of e-learning and can acquire competence and confidence in the new skills they will need.

These assertions lead to a model of strategy implementation that looks at:

- what management must put in place to initiate and support change
- how it can enable individual staff to change
- how staff and learners can change their practice
- how to bring this together to change the organisation as a whole.

Delivering the promise:
A four-stage model of change

The 'Delivering the promise' model identifies a sequence of actions that must be taken by management to start the ball rolling, maintain momentum and hand over to individual practitioners the wherewithal to enable them make effective use of technology for learning and teaching in all of its forms.

It is a model of delivery of strategy rather than of strategy creation. Its starting point is the organisation's e-learning strategy. Strategy will change as circumstances change. Government policy, funding constraints, student numbers, social, cultural and technological developments must all be accommodated by reviewing and revising the organisation's strategy. Each time this happens, the organisation should go through the four stages of the model to ensure that it can deliver the promise of the new strategy.

The four stages are:
Stage 1. The foundations for change
Stage 2. Change the individual
Stage 3. Change practice
Stage 4. Change the organisation

In the centre of the diagram is a target representing the goal, with teaching and learning practice at its heart. The outer rings represent the key structures that must be put in place to get the organisation to this goal:

- a vision of where it wants to be with e-learning and a strategy to get it there
- the computing and communications infrastructure of kit, connectivity and appropriate content for staff and learners to use
- staff development programmes and opportunities.

Delivering the promise model: Overview

Stage1: The foundations for change

Strategic investments, assets and enablers

The foundations for turning vision into practice consist of a number of distinctive strategic assets, most notably a robust technical infrastructure and a capacity for developing staff skills. Typically they will include:

- **management structure, responsibilities and roles.**
- **communications infrastructure**
- **computers and connectivity**
- **a learning platform.**

Stage2: Change the individual

When the foundations are in place, individual staff can be made ready to deliver the strategy. They must be:

- made aware of the vision and strategy,
- trained in the skills they need
  - given the time, support and access to become competent and confident.

The service must
  - **communicate the vision**
  - **train and support staff**
  - **ensure availability of resources and access to computers and other kit.**

Staff must understand the vision, know what it means for them and their learners and get the skills to deliver it

Stage 3: Change practice

Armed with skills and the necessary equipment, staff can begin to develop practice by exploring curriculum, teaching and learning opportunities – supported by enthusiasts like E Guides.

The key here is **staff enablement.**

This means the service must ensure that staff who have undertaken training now have:

- **schedules that allow development time**
- **access to appropriate resources, equipment and support**
- use of a learning platform.

Stage 4: Change the organisation

The organisation changes when the actions of individual staff and learners move beyond novelty into mainstream activity. Skills and practice come together with **development, discovery, adaptation and sharing of curriculum content and activities.**

Staff and learners can build communities of practice – ideally through **a learning platform,** whose full value is now realised.

The role of management is to:

- **recognise and reward staff through observation and appraisal**
- **sustain and develop infrastructure and resources**
- **consolidate the use of external expertise (e.g. RSCs).**
- Recognise and reward learners' involvement in organisational strategy

Bob Powell (2008)

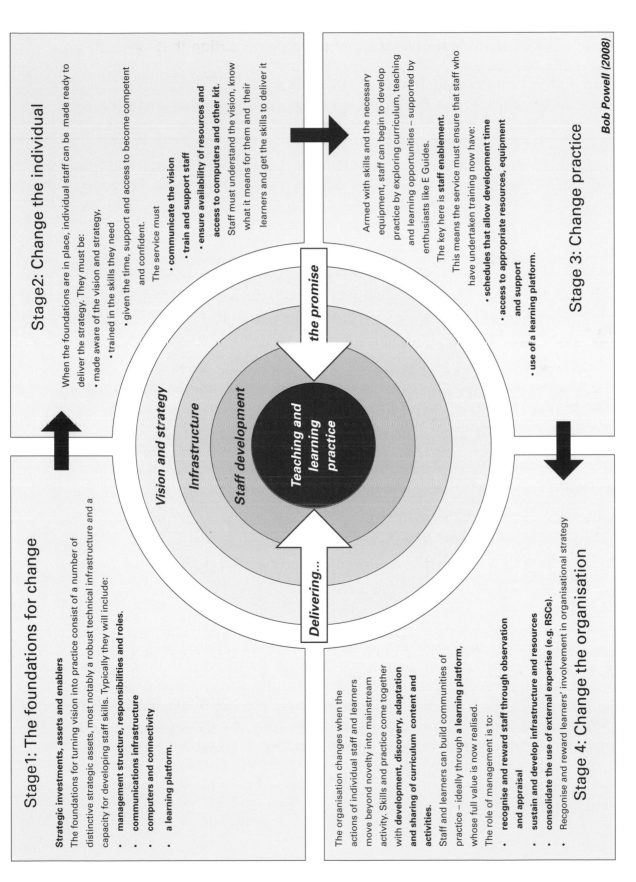

Vision and strategy

Infrastructure

Staff development

Teaching and learning practice

the promise

Delivering...

Stage 1. The foundations for change

Before anything can happen that will move the organisation towards delivering its vision for e-learning, the management team must have a strategy for e-learning, translated into an action plan, and the technical infrastructure necessary to facilitate appropriate levels of activity by staff. All the activity at this stage is management-driven. In practice we may find that small numbers of individual enthusiasts have already developed their own islands of practice, but these will have little impact on the organisation as a whole if there is no overall management direction and the foundations are not in place.

The most obvious element of the foundations is the computing and communications infrastructure required to deliver the proposed levels of access and activity. In most organisations this infrastructure will include a learning platform, whether it is a web portal, an intranet or a Virtual Learning Environment (VLE).

In Bournemouth Adult Learning, the adult learning service demonstrated that use of a VLE made significant improvements in its staff development programme, the provision of e-learning support and teaching resources for both staff and learners and in the free flow of information across the Service.

Equally important, however, is a management structure of roles and responsibilities, led by senior management, with:

- a clear brief to deliver the strategy
- an action plan to schedule key tasks
- a budget for the necessary investment, including staff time
- a review and self-assessment process
- a staff development structure and plan.

The overarching group should encompass those with a responsibility for supporting staff development and any e-learning champions in the Service, that is, individuals that take on the role of working with their peers to encourage and support e-learning practice. In adult learning, the national programme for individuals wishing to adopt an e-learning champion role is known as the E-Guides Programme (see 'Further information', p. 48). Involving your E-Guides at an early stage will ensure that they are well-informed about the strategy and motivated to see it work in practice. They will also be an authoritative source of feedback on progress, achievements and challenge.

The value of E-Guides has been demonstrated in York. The City of York Adult Education Council trained six E-Guides who then went on to provide e-learning related peer support to fifty other staff in e-learning, helped train over one hundred and twenty staff in accessing the Service's VLE. In addition to the role of the E-Guides, the post of 'e-learning support tutor' was established to provide 'Just in Time' (JIT) training.

Stage 2. Change the individual

Once the foundations for change are in place, the next step is to encourage and enable individual staff to contribute fully. Managers need to communicate the vision effectively, so that staff knows what is expected of them and for what purpose. They must be made aware of the organisation's vision and strategy for e-learning, be trained and prepared to carry out the necessary tasks and then acquire competence and confidence in the relevant skills through repetition and practice.

The City of York Adult Education Council communicated its vision across the Service through a variety of activities including the use of staff newsletters, the organisation of curriculum groups and delivery of staff development training sessions. In fact, staff development sessions underpin all genuine innovation, but will succeed only if individuals have the time and motivation to develop the skills to which training programmes introduce them.

Stage 3. Change practice

Armed with skills and access to equipment staff can begin to innovate and to improve practice by exploring the curriculum, teaching and learning opportunities that technology opens up. Many organisations train large numbers of staff at great expense, but fail to take the next step of **enablement**

Staff are trained if they have the skills to do something; they are enabled if management ensures that they also have sufficient time to apply those skills and appropriate access to the equipment they need. The experience of Bournemouth Adult Learning showed that there is a great deal of support and training available to members of staff but too little time to enable them to fit what they learned into busy lives.

Equally important, if practice is to change, is support for tutors and learners at the point of delivery so as to relieve the anxiety of those risky first attempts at embedding technology into teaching and learning.

Stage 4. Change the organisation

Changing the organisation means transforming delivery, learner experience and outcomes. It requires the individual actions of staff to move beyond novelty and pioneering and into mainstream practice. E-learning demands the acquisition not only of a set of skills and access to infrastructure, but also the development, discovery, adaptation and adoption of a critical mass of online content, activities, links and sources.

This works most effectively when staff takes the step from individual endeavour to sharing good practice with colleagues. The staff at Portsmouth Adult and Community Learning has embraced good practice in many lessons and across an increasing number of courses due to joint working across 4 local authorities in the area sharing skills and good practice. They have also been able to create a pool of resources, both hardware and software for loan.

The role of management now is to create a structure that recognises and rewards staff for engaging with e-learning. This will usually take the form of building it into teaching observation and appraisal.

Few organisations have managed to get very far down the road of change without making good use of the expertise of agencies and institutions such as NIACE and the British Education and Communications Technology Agency (Becta), the latter of which is funded by government to promote and support e-learning as part of its brief, as well as partnerships and shared working with peer institutions.

'Delivering the promise' model: Organisation and individual perspectives

Managers can make decisions, create plans, take actions and set up structures, but to no purpose unless individual tutors, administrators and support staff respond appropriately. As we have already observed, management is about getting *other* people to do things.

Delivering the strategy, therefore, requires separate, but inter-related actions by:

* the management of the organisation

* each individual.

* The learner

This second representation of the model separates:

* the actions of the organisation's managers and the enablers they have available to them to bring about change

* the changes they are trying to bring about in individual teachers, other staff and in learners.

Management effort is heaviest at the start of the process, as it moves individuals through awareness and understanding, supports the development of skills and provides infrastructure and motivation. It then steps back as practitioners pick up the reins and drive their own curriculum and learners forward.

This is not the end of management input however. Technology continues to change and as a result so too do the possibilities it offers to improve the experience and achievement of learners. A critical function of management is to sustain the investment, to replace and reinvigorate the assets and to begin the cycle afresh whenever the vision or the context in which it must be delivered changes.

'Delivering the Promise' model: Individual and organisational perspectives

	Individual		Organisation	
	Goal	Action	Action	Enabler
Stage 1. The foundations for change				
			Understand the possibilities	Vision
			Create management structure	Strategy
			Set realistic goals, timescales, budget	Action plan
			Acquire kit and connectivity	Infrastructure
Stage 2. Change the individual				
Become:	Aware	Listen	Tell them/ get their attention	Communication: effort, media
	Able	Try, do	Show them how, train	E-Guides training, a staff development programme
	Competent	Repeat and practice	Support staff and learners	Time, access, support

Stage 3. Change practice				
Take action	Develop	Explore opportunities	Enable	Time, access, support
	Change teaching change learning	Apply skills	Empower	A curriculum change programme, Involving the learners
Stage 4 Change the organisation				
Joint action	Work together	Share, collaborate	Provide incentives, disseminate good practice	A common learning platform Observation programme
	Communities of practice	Synthesise, belong	Encourage recognise and reward	Curriculum
	Mainstream	Just another tool	Measure, monitor review – and repeat the cycle	Appraisal, ongoing assessment of learners – both for learning and of learning

Management structure, responsibilities and roles

The management structure of roles, responsibilities and reporting processes is what will:

- drive investment
- steer and monitor activity
- ensure that things stay on track.

Delivering the Promise

Many organisations already have created a steering group or committee to produce or oversee the writing of the strategy. Others have ad hoc steering groups or nominated individuals responsible for funded projects, which have been a significant source of capital for many cash-strapped services. The remit of these groups must be reviewed and amended as necessary to reflect the new role. Implementing an institution wide strategy is not the same task as writing one or managing a focused project.

There are a small number of critical elements that make for an effective management structure to deliver e-learning strategy in practice:

1. Have a nominated manager with responsibility for e-learning strategy and development, ideally as their sole job function.

2. Include significant senior management presence, either in numbers or rank.

3. Recognise and reflect the needs of the larger organisation to which the service reports and ultimately, the overarching Authority.

4. Include, or call upon sufficient technical e-learning expertise to guide its decisions.

5. Include or collect the views of practitioners – academic, administrative and technical.

A dedicated manager for e-learning

Many consultants believe that creating a dedicated management post is the single most influential factor in driving e-learning forward in a Service. It is a highly practical way to ensure the effective delivery of strategy, particularly if you can employ a person full time in the role, because:

- the role-holder devotes their entire working week to developing e-learning

- the pre-existing skills, knowledge and enthusiasm that won the job are reinforced and extended.

E-learning is no different from any other specialist area of work in this regard: getting the right person with the right skills and potential and giving them responsibility for doing a specific job is always likely to be more effective than piling additional responsibilities onto an existing post-holder. Such a position can only come into existence, moreover, if two other critical foundations for success are in place

- senior management commitment to developing e-learning

- funding to support e-learning development.

A dedicated post is unlikely to repay its salary by cutting costs or bringing in revenue, though it may lead to better bids for external project money, or even be funded out of project income. The real return to the organisation is in the increased effectiveness with which strategy is delivered and practice is supported and developed.

Most services either cannot, or choose not to, fund a dedicated post in the face of more immediate pressures competing for finance out of the same restricted pot of money. E-learning is not *toothache urgent* for managers, unlike issues such as restructuring or any number of politically driven initiatives and agendas. Delivering an e-learning strategy, however, demands that where responsibility for e-learning is included as one of many different duties in a wider management post – increasingly the norm in a world of reorganisation – it is a valued and important part of the role, not just an add-on to the job description.

Emerging practice in such cases has seen a shift to including it in the brief of managers responsible for curriculum and quality issues. This is clearly best practice when the end point of e-learning strategy is to improve teaching and learning.

Even a dedicated post for e-learning development will not have an impact unless the management structure takes into account the second assertion: management is not about doing things *per se*, but getting others in the organisation to change their practice. The e-learning manager can only deliver change with the support of line managers, so getting them on board is essential. It also requires on-theground assistance from E-Guides or their equivalent, who are an integral part of an effective management structure.

Senior Management engagement

E-learning is not usually introduced into a service by its Senior Management Team (SMT), though there are some notably enthusiastic Heads of Service in adult learning. It has not been high on the SMT agenda in most services recently, in the face of more urgent matters, such as the redirection of funding priorities and the difficulties of consequent restructuring.

Government policy has been the major driver in raising e-learning onto the SMT agenda in post-16 education nationally and in providing capital to pump-prime infrastructure development. Policymakers have not imposed measurable targets or monitored outcomes for e-learning at the level of the individual organisation and it has not, until recently, been subject to active scrutiny by the inspection regime, so there has been little to grab SMT attention and enforce action.

Individual enthusiasts amongst the teaching staff are often responsible for much of the initial impetus and continuing drive for development. In many schools, colleges and Services the difference between departments or sites in terms of e-learning activity can be explained wholly by reference to a small number of enthusiasts. It is almost a truism and certainly unarguable, however, that active SMT support is essential if the strategy is to be delivered across the organisation, rather than patchily implemented in a series of trench-by-trench battles, or – even worse – indifference.

This is not the place to rehearse the reasons why SMT should concern itself with e-learning; a good summary of the arguments can be found in the management modules of the NIACE Staff development e-learning centre (SDELC) website (see 'Further information', p. 49). In the context of delivering the e-learning strategy, however, a lack of management support is fatal.

Engaging the wider organisation

Adult learning services often sit in the middle of two forces. Above them is the overarching body that is the wider Authority, which sets policy, controls finance and regulates practice. On the other side are the delivery partners, including both direct deliverers of learning and those who provide accommodation and support. The impact on e-learning strategy can be overwhelming. The Authority may already have a strategy for learning and technology across all of its education activities, which set the framework, and parameters for the Service's own strategy, including corporate ICT policies, which restrict the freedom to choose and use particular technical solutions. On the delivery side are autonomous organisations with their own priorities and strategies.

All of these bodies must be engaged if the strategy is to be delivered. Proper consultation when putting together a vision statement and strategy is essential to produce an achievable development programme. During the delivery phase, which we are concerned with here, success will depend upon being able to get these other autonomous elements of the wider organisation to engage with the strategy and do what is necessary to deliver it.

Stage 1: Foundations for change

A review and self-assessment process

A formal management structure with a dedicated post responsible for e-learning sets the framework for converting strategic intention into practice. The management team must be able to identify and assess progress in each key area of the strategy against the measurable targets and milestones contained in the Action Plan. These form the basis for monitoring, measuring, reporting and reviewing delivery of the strategy.

In practice there are two approaches that can be taken to this:

1. Assign responsibility for separate areas to individual staff or teams and leave them to collect quantitative and qualitative data as they see fit to report back to the management group.

2. Use a common review and assessment tool to systematise the collection, recording and presentation of data.

The first method is the one that most organisations appear to use. This seems to work well for services with realistic and achievable action plans, disseminated to key staff and well understood throughout the organisation. The effort of information gathering is spread between staff and is absorbed into daily practice and it fits comfortably with standard authority- or service-wide procedures and documents.

The use of a formal tool is time-consuming and therefore needs to be seen to add value to the management of strategy in order to justify the resource allocated to it. There are a number of organisational self-review tools being used in adult learning and a common feature of all the tools is that they break down information and communications technology (ICT) and e-learning into categories or descriptors, against which the Service can then self assess.

Such self-review tools cover areas that are about vision and strategic planning; teaching and learning; staff development; infrastructure and equipment; and managing and implementing ICT and e-learning. An immediate advantage to the organisation of using a dedicated e-learning self-review tool comes from reassurance that it identifies and addresses all of the key areas, so nothing major is left out or overlooked. One assessment and review device that has been used in further education colleges is the National Learning Network (NLN) Transformation Tool (see 'Further information', p. 48).

Those services that have used a self-review tool value it as a device for helping to delivery strategy. It can be used:

- as a measure of the current state of e-learning infrastructure, capability, management and practice, providing not only an initial benchmark against which to measure and review progress, but also a red light on key elements of the foundations for change which are absent, or inadequate to provide a base for development;

- as a time scheduled statement of the end goals.

In addition, self-review can be used to raise staff awareness of the issues associated with implementing ICT/e-learning and when used as part of staff development programmes, can be used as a source document for discussion or to engage staff in putting together an organisational review.

When Bromley Adult Education College completed its e-learning self-review, it identified that the college was generally at a 'developing' stage in terms of its e-learning practice. Bromley then revised its e-learning strategy, following the NIACE e-strategy guidelines, and included within it an action plan to move the college forward.

The effort put into any self-review process is rewarded by the value it adds to the planning process. Used properly, it can assist in the setting of priorities, timescales and budgets. It also functions as an internal monitoring and planning tool, a benchmark against other Services and to support preparation for inspection.

Becta has supported the use of a variety of ICT and e-learning self-review tools (see Further information, p. 48) and is striving to develop a common ICT and e-learning self-review framework for all those sectors that operate beyond compulsory education in the United Kingdom. The adoption of one common tool enables organisations to measure their development towards the goal of seamless use of technology for learning and management, and to compare their progress against other providers.

A structure for staff development

All three of the assertions that underpin the 'Delivering promise' model point to the need to put in place a structure for staff development as a foundation for change. It is fundamental to the success of the next two stages of the model: Changing the individual and Changing practice. If we look at the job to be done in those stages we can see that the staff development structure is required to do more than simply identify courses to send staff on.

The building blocks of an effective staff development structure to deliver e-learning strategy are:

- access to expertise on staff development needs and solutions
- a budget, both for formal training programmes and for ensuing development activity
- a framework of support mechanisms for individual staff.

The E-Guides programme

The two major sources of expertise available to Services are:

- the JISC Regional Support Centres (RSC), who are funded to work with the further education (FE) colleges and adult learning services in their area
- E-Guides, champions and enthusiasts within the organisation.

The sheer numbers of client organisations in a region restrict the scale and nature of the personal support that RSCs can deliver to any given organisation. They are able to provide advice and guidance on programmes and courses and to share experience of what has worked elsewhere in the region and nationally for similar organisations to your own. They are also a major broker of training courses and awareness events.

The need for on-the-spot in-house expertise was one of the drivers that led NIACE to devise the E-Guides programme. It enables organisations to develop the skills and knowledge of a cadre of selected practitioners, who can then guide and support colleagues in their own use of technology for learning. It is designed to sit at the heart of a structured staff development programme in which the E-Guides cascade their training to coach and to mentor colleagues. The national E-Guides training programme develops skills in the use of learning technologies and provides resources to support colleagues who are developing e-learning.

Trained E-Guides constitute one of the most significant strategic assets within the organisation because of their potential to move staff forward. It is essential that they are appropriately selected and used effectively. Few organisations feel able to make the post full-time or provide any financial incentive. This does not seem to deter a steady stream of enthusiastic and committed professionals who find adequate reward in helping colleagues in a varied and interesting set of challenges and in having access to a comprehensive kit of equipment and resources.

Many services, at least initially, encouraged volunteers to train as e-Guides. At **Plymouth City Council** the E-Guides training was a starting point for the formation of an ICT and e-learning Strategy. Tracy Hewett, the Senior Adult Education Officer comments:

> A critical factor in the success of E-Guides is to find people who you think would be useful and to be realistic about people's abilities. E-Guides should be approached and not necessarily be self-referring.

The attrition rate of E-Guides nationally, however, has been fairly large. This has been for many causes, not least that volunteers may be motivated by the prospect of career movement that the new skills may provide. Some have been lost to reorganisation, whilst others have decided it is not for them. The drop out, given the relatively small numbers of E-Guides in any given service, can be important.

The strategic challenge for management is to retain the knowledge and capability within the service even if the E-Guide moves on. Trained E-Guides are a significant strategic asset in the staff development structure.

One answer is for managers to accept that training new Guides is a critical investment that is likely to recur. The other is to ensure that training genuinely cascades through the organisation, from E-Guide to tutor and on from that tutor to the next, that is, to ensure that a community of practice builds and shares expertise.

An Example: Portsmouth City Council

Portsmouth City Council is a good example of a Service that put sound foundations for change in place to develop and deliver its e-learning strategy. These include:

- senior management support
- engagement of the wider organisation
- a structure for staff development
- funding
- expertise in e-learning in the planning group.

The council is relatively small unitary authority with some fairly deprived neighbourhoods and wards. Steve Glennon has responsibility for the overall direction of e-learning within a wider brief and the words quoted here are his.

He attributes the significant progress that Portsmouth has made with e-learning to a good strategy, put together following a trip with the Head of Service to

> ... a conference at Milton Keynes... as a result of that we came back absolutely enthused

They quickly identified two colleagues who combined specific expertise in ICT and e-learning with experience and understanding of the service and could make a significant contribution to planning and development.

> Having some experts to help you write the Strategy and to know what it is that your Service does and where it wants to go. It's quite critical to having a good Strategy.

Working together the four produced the first draft of Portsmouth's ICT and e-learning strategy. Following subsequent refinement and revision the strategy was adopted by the City Council as its authority-wide strategy for e-learning. This meant not only senior management support from the Head of Service, but also the engagement of the wider Authority.

A steering group was set up to oversee development of the strategy and its implementation. This is broadly based, with representation from all key stakeholder groups including members of other City Council directorates, contracted learning providers, members of the IT Services Group, and a couple of other interested parties. The group works to disseminate and share information across the organisation and to feed back on issues and developments.

The structure is focused upon the purpose of the organisation (in line with assertion 1 of the Delivering Promise model):

> ...we monitor with our contracted providers the extent to which they are implementing e-learning, having impact with e-learning in teaching and learning.

Staff development was identified from the outset as one of three fundamental drivers for strategy.

> One thing we came away from the Milton Keynes conference is that everything is connected like a triangle – with connectivity, content development and continuing professional development as the corner stones of ... what we're going to do within the strategy. We have made some real progress on developing staff and on content development as they've been lots of opportunities nationally for this.

The staff development structure makes use of the commitment to E-Guides, who are a key channel for communicating and implementing strategy. As a small authority, Portsmouth has difficulty finding the budget to deliver change. They have adopted two successful approaches:

1. Bidding for external funding. The key to this has been the initial e-learning strategy:

> *I think the other thing is that because we started with a solid foundation as a good Strategy document it's stood us in good stead every time we've applied for funding. We can point to that as the driver – it's that I'm sure that is taken into consideration when funds are allocated and whenever we pitch for funds we pitch for funds that are linked to the strategy and the action plan.*

2. Working in partnership with colleagues in neighbouring authorities. Association with Southampton, Isle of Wight and Hampshire has enabled Portsmouth to join in a successful European Social Fund (ESF) project 'E-into ACL' led by the Isle of Wight.

> *As a small City Council it is fairly important for us to work in partnerships with others colleagues as we'd simply not have enough resources to do the work we do and make progress… were it not for successfully bidding for funds and pots of money like TrEACL and E-Shift and so on we would be far further behind than where we are now. The level of resourcing of a small authority like mine simply would not have been able to stretch – we wouldn't have been able to fund resources and buy in trainers and managers.*

[TrEACL and E-Shift was the provision of e-learning funding by the Learning and Skills Council via NIACE to the community-based adult learning sector.]

Making staff aware: Communicating the vision and strategy

Once the foundations for change are in place, work can begin to with the individual staff whose change in practice is the end goal. In reality these separate strands will overlap. It is unlikely that any organisation will wait until everything is in place before telling staff what is going on and what it is trying to achieve. There is an underlying truth, however, that until the foundations for change of infrastructure and support are in place any attempt to develop staff will be hampered.

We are working on the well-founded assertion that staff want to do their best for learners and so will be willing to adopt new practices that will be beneficial to learners. However, we accept that they will require support to do this.

The first step on the road to changing the perspective and practice of individual staff is telling them what the organisation is trying to do. This involves communicating the vision and strategy to staff, and begs the question as to what is the best way to get your message across.

Visions do not communicate well. They focus on future possibilities and hopes and it can be difficult for those who have them in their mind to transfer the picture unambiguously and with clarity into words. The communication problem is compounded, no matter how brilliant is the translation of vision into words, by the fact that each listener may see a very picture in their own mind. The strategy documents, action plans and the e-learning self-review tools are all useful, but it is unwise to rely upon staff taking it all in just because they have been told about it.

A number of options for communicating the proposals for e-learning are seen in practice, ranging from notifying people at meetings or in writing, demonstrating or showing aspects, sharing artefacts, asking questions or inviting contributions and various methods for intriguing or engaging the attention of staff.

Many organisations are content to rely upon Microsoft PowerPoint presentations and a handout at staff meetings. Copies of these and related information may be held on an intranet, for example, where staff can seek it out afterwards. It is interesting to note that this approach would not be acceptable to practitioners if the target audience were learners; the inspectorate would not accept that real learning had taken place if there were no reinforcement or testing of understanding.

The most effective way to communicate the vision is to ensure that staff is required to respond to the information with an action or activity that will help to make it meaningful to them. In general, successful approaches to communication look to use a combination of media and methods and to stimulate understanding through activity, whether that be through discussion of the issues or actually delivering an outcome in response.

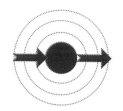

Stage 2: Change the individual

Developing staff

The aim of the strategy is to change teaching and learning practise. When staff have been made aware of what the organisation is trying to achieve, then the next step is to ensure that individual tutors can acquire the skills and understanding that they need in order to rethink, adapt and change their practice.

A programme of staff development must have the following elements if it is to be effective in bringing about a change in practice:

- training opportunities
- time and access to equipment for staff to reinforce training and build competence and confidence
- support for individuals and groups

Training opportunities

Staff training is the one area that most people agree is essential, not surprisingly for organisations whose raison d'etre is education and training. Getting members of staff together to undertake training is notoriously difficult. Matters are made even more difficult in adult learning organisations by the fact that a majority of teachers are part time or sessional members of staff that are often on short hour contracts.

> *"Compared to the time that a typical tutor might spend in teaching their subject, training in or even just discussing ICT is a considerable investment in time".*

[Implementing e-learning in ACL provision: findings from community based adult learning service providers' e-strategy reviews. Lindsay research & consulting, NIACE 2007].

They may require payment for attending training sessions.
> *"It's a big ask for tutors to take a day off to come on training courses"*
[Paul Kelly, Cheshire]

They may, moreover, be distributed between multiple sites across the country.
> *"It is only possible to train small numbers at any one time, so skills dissemination necessarily proceeds at a slow pace."*
[Phil Hardcastle, Leicester County Council and now independent consultant].

There is external pressure on staff to secure their professional status by updating now that the Institute for Learning requires annual continuing professional development (CPD) for all staff, from a minimum of 6 hours per year for those on the shortest contracted hours to 30 hours for full time staff.

Staff enablement

All too often the hard work and cost of organising a training programme and getting everyone together to take part does not take the organisation forward as expected, particularly in the application of technology to learning which takes many staff out of their comfort zone.

> *We have run three full training days over the past year with little discernible impact on what staff actually does. They like it, they enjoy the day and using the equipment but it doesn't carry through into practice*

Training courses alone will never have lasting impact on what staff does in the classroom with e-learning, no matter how good the course, unless there are opportunities for reinforcement and practice afterwards. Courses can turn out to be like a bee-sting: a dramatic instant response that rapidly fades without fresh input.

Stimulating, well-run courses are good at raising awareness, calming initial fears, introducing skills and motivating staff to do more, but unless time and access to equipment is provided afterwards that enables staff to practice, levels of competence and confidence are likely to be too low for many staff to risk trying them out in practice.

The term *staff enablement* is helpful because it allows us to separate what the organisation can do from what the individuals must do for themselves:

The organisation can train staff, but it cannot develop them

Tutors have to develop their own competence and confidence in the new skills and work out for themselves how they can adopt and adapt them into their own practice. The organisation can *enable* this to happen by ensuring time and access to equipment.

The lack of time and resource for reinforcing and developing skills and understanding is why training courses generally do not bring about the transformation in teaching and learning practice that managers hope for, even when the feedback on the day is that the course was excellent. This is almost certainly the most significant explanation of why e-learning strategy proceeds at a slower pace than we would wish.

An example:
Cheshire Lifelong Learning Service

Cheshire Lifelong Learning Service (CLLS) is a good example of a Service that has worked hard to prepare individual staff to contribute to delivery of the e-learning strategy. It is wholly contracted-out service managed by Cheshire County Council with over 30,000 enrolments a year.

CLLS has worked to address each of the main elements of phase two of the model:

- communicate the vision

- train and support staff

- ensure availability of resources and access to computers and other kit.

CLLS put in place some important foundations to support change:

1. Progress is monitored regularly against the strategy and action plan, making use of an organisational e-learning self-review tool known as the ACL eLPs (the adult and community learning e-learning positioning statement tool – see 'Further information', p. 48) to measure distance travelled.

2. The appointment of a dedicated Learning Technology manager, Paul Kelly, whose remit was to re-write and implement the e-learning strategy, and whose comments are quoted here.

Communicating the vision

The revised ICT and e-learning strategy was written around six key priorities:

- training and development opportunities for all staff

- increased engagement and use of the CLLS Learning Platform

- increased blended and distance learning opportunities

- ICT to be utilised in all aspects of leadership and management

- quality resources available for staff to enable effective use of ICT in teaching and learning.

- an awareness campaign to raise the profile of ICT in teaching and learning.
  Getting this Vision over – after all it's a 60 page document – has been difficult and what we've come up with is a shortened summary which was a 4-page A5 flyer that we were able to send out in the tutor packs which has highlighted the six priorities and has been very well received. All of

our tutors get a copy of this on an annual basis and this primarily has been the way we've communicated the vision although we do have an annual conference and this is an opportunity to champion the work of ICT. We've been very successful with some projects and this is a way to tell everyone about it. But with a commissioned-out model it is sometimes difficult and it's a long haul. We have to be realistic.

CLLS used money from an E-Shift bid (see p. 20) to run a one-day staff development programme, involving 100 tutors who were paid £10 per hour to attend. The programme gave:

... a flavour of what ICT is all about, how it can impact on them as tutors and more important how it could impact on the learners.

It was an experiential day where the delegates had a curriculum-based project to complete during the day, supported by trainers. Tutors were:

... let loose in a safe environment. The feedback at the end of the day showed that the predominant reason people don't use the equipment is the fear of failure. So that's what we set out to do at the event – to try and help them get over their fear. We got a huge intake from that and that really made a platform for us to kick on.

An online staff training course hosted on the learning platform supplements face to face events. Paul Kelly recognises that the impact of training cannot be gauged by the positive feedback on the day:

We measure impact by getting feedback on the day – but it just measures whether people are happy. We are putting in place a continuing programme of staff observation that sees if it carries through.

The service has a systematic teaching observation process, which can identify and focus on tutors who came onto the course over the next 3 years to see if they carry use of ICT into the learning situation. Early results are mixed: some do, some don't.

As a contracted out service, CLLS can deliver centralised training with access to excellent resources on the day, but economic constraints in some delivery partners mean there is insufficient equipment and therefore little opportunity for practice. A problem remains finding a budget for training when project funding runs out:

What we're finding is that as we can't pay tutors to come along it's a big ask to have a day off especially if they need to find other work as they're part time tutors.

Stage 3: Change Practice

Learning platforms

The most significant step for many services when seeking to move from the independent innovation of a few staff to an organisation wide change of teaching and learning practice is to implement a learning platform.

The most familiar forms of learning platform in adult learning are Virtual Learning Environments (VLEs), intranets and web portals.

They are used to create, adapt and store learning materials and resources, to organise and structure learning pathways or courses and to act as the main communication system for the organisation. They bring teachers and learners together around what appears to the user to be a single place.

A learning platform is characterised by a common front end and navigation tools that bring consistency, coherence and a sense of shared community and common purpose to what would otherwise be a loose tangle of independent activity by individual tutors and learners, each using their own preferred designs, delivery approaches and media.

Over the typical three-year lifespan of a strategic plan for e-learning, a learning platform can become the core of changing practice in teaching and learning. The name of the platform – either the proprietary title of the product or the organisation's own chosen term – often becomes shorthand for e-learning in the organisation. This has both positive and negative aspects.

The greatest positive is that all tutors and all learners have a shared understanding of where to go and what to expect and a shared set of terms to describe it. The negative is if it makes people overlook other, non platform-based activities.

In practice this does not seem to happen; building e-learning around a learning platform appears to stimulate the use of technology for learning in all its forms. For reasons such as this, most adult learning providers now have a learning platform or are in the process of implementing one.

Ironically, its impact on the face to face teaching and learning that constitutes the vast majority of educational experience is likely to be far less in the short term than whole class presentation equipment such as electronic whiteboards, data projectors or presentation software and, at an individual learner level, the use of digital cameras and a range of handheld devices.

The most common uses of the Internet, such as information searching, do not need a learning platform and no-one really expects large amounts of freestanding online learning content to be developed that will rely solely upon a learning platform for its delivery. Delivery of content online usually requires human support.

As an asset for driving strategic change in teaching and learning practice, however, a learning platform is an essential investment. There is no other tool that so visibly delivers:

• coherence of activity	Teaching and learning practice, activities and information are all pulled together around a single place.
• commonality and sharing	It is the place to share e-learning resources and to work together and to communicate.
• consistency of practice	Everyone uses the same platform and develops the same skills set, no matter how individual and distinctive are the solutions and resources they develop and use within it.

A learning platform can bind the whole e-learning strategy together in the minds of tutors and learners if it becomes the single place where both tutors and learners consistently go to find messages, course documents, information, materials and activities.

Practice changes tangibly – and measurably – when the platform becomes the first port of call. All of the more visible manifestations of e-learning practice will link into the platform, either as stored outcomes (digital photos embedded into text documents or presentations for example), source materials for presentations and individual activity, or as a channel for information and communication. Hartlepool Adult and Community learning, for example, is in partnership with other local authorities in the region on the development of a Tees Valley Moodle. Moodle is one type of learning platform (see 'Further information', p. 48).

There has been extensive staff training on the creation and use of the Moodle as well as a number of sessions on the use of information and communications technology in teaching. Members of staff from the Service are working with colleagues from other Services in the Tees Valley to produce e-learning material. The service has broadband connectivity via the Joint Academic

Network (JANET) (see 'Further information', p. 48) and further use of JANET is planned to enable learners to access their own e-mail accounts. At the moment, learners can access content, including assessment, online via both Hartlepool's own learning platform and the Tees Valley joint Moodle website.

The key question in our context of delivering the promise is what you have to do to get it used. In practice this means how you get teachers and learners to use the learning platform. Engaging teachers is particularly important because they must be the ones to set up and structure activities for learners and steer them onto it.

The acquisition and implementation of a learning platform and its subsequent absorption into everyday practice will itself follow the stages of the 'Delivering the promise' model we have looked at: from installation and implementation – setting the foundation for change, through staff awareness and skills raising, until confident users take advantage of the opportunities for sharing and building the communities of practice that characterise embedding into mainstream practice.

Learning platforms and staff practice

One of the more telling contributions that a learning platform can make is to the whole process of staff engagement with e-learning. Consultant Terry Loane, an expert on Moodle who has worked with many services says:

I'm a firm believer that the way for an organisation to implement a learning platform successfully is to start using it for staff development. When staff uses a learning platform as a learner they can quickly gain confidence and they will start using it with their own learners.

This is increasingly common. A variant is to be found at Bournemouth Adult Learning, who encouraged staff to use the Moodle learning platform by embedding it into its teacher training programmes. Bournemouth believes that if tutors use the environment as a learner at an early stage, they will be much more likely to bring it through into their own teaching.

Course leaders found that tutors liked what the system offered and how easy it was to use, but noticed that after the training there was not much follow-up activity. One-to-one sessions were introduced to supplement the tuition and help to reinforce use of the platform. There seems no short-cutting the slow process of development from awareness, through the gathering of ability to enablement and eventual changed practice.

An example: Getting the learning platform used

Chris Kemp, an Information and Learning Technology (ILT) Co-ordinator at Middlesbrough Adult Education Service has been very successful in getting the Service's Moodle platform used and accepted by both learners and teachers.

I want to talk about three things. The first is how to engage reluctant tutors. With our service we have some success with engaging reluctant tutors mainly through peer pressure and that's not just peer pressure from other tutors but it's also pressure from the learners. How we have dealt with this is we have marketed to the learners that ... an online classroom will become available and within this classroom you can access resources for your course.

It works something like this as not every course is online. If you ask your tutor they may be able to point you in the right direction. This 'ask your tutor' bit has triggered off for many tutors to come to us and ask for an online course. So it's worked really well.

The other thing that has worked quite well is that when we deliver training we deliver to curriculum groups so say if a curriculum group got together I'd actually hijack half the meeting to talk about ICT and the VLE. When you get a whole group of tutors together, say the language tutors, it's really good to see how they are using the VLE– how audio or video has been brought in to their teaching. It's encouraged the rest of the tutors.

The same for other areas – it works for Arts and Crafts too.

The third thing is that as every learner walks through the door we provide a login on an information card about the Online Classroom – everyone got it if they wanted it or not. It also says on the card again 'ask your tutor'.

This route is backed up by the support and the opportunity to develop skills. All of the attempts to develop teaching and learning practice have the enablement focus, insofar as they combine providing equipment for previously trained staff, in the classroom, with support from an E-Guide or equivalent mentor either in the classroom or beforehand, as appropriate.

Middlesbrough has been part of a couple of projects in partnership with other Services in the region to develop Moodle as a shared and jointly developed platform for learning, teaching and communication, with all of the Heads of Service actively involved in the steering groups.

Teaching practice

It is a big step for staff to go from a one-off training event to applying skills in the learning situation. We know, however, that there is a great deal of teaching and learning going on that makes use of digital technology and also that learners are increasingly using it at home or in libraries and other centres, which tells us that many staff have already made or are making this step.

Setting targets

The standard management tool for achieving a goal is to convert it into targets that staff can understand and aim for. In the case of e-learning this is particularly difficult, not least because the whole point of using technology for learning is not to do it for its own sake but because – and where – it will improve the learning experience and learning outcomes. The people who are best placed to make this decision are the teachers and learners.

We have already noted that teachers are unwilling to take risks with the learner outcomes and arbitrary targets are not going to overcome this. It is the teachers who must make the change once they are helped to see the benefits and supported in being enabled to deliver them.

A sensible alternative to formal targets which will help to move staff towards the use of e-learning, however, and which has other benefits as we shall see later, is to announce that e-learning will be included as an element in observed teaching sessions, by agreement with tutors. This will gently set the requirement, raising both tutor awareness and demand for the services of the E-Guides.

Support for staff

Having trained staff and enabled them to refine their skills, the next step is to carry this forward into:

- the development of curriculum practice
- use in the learning situation.

This is where E-Guides can be expected to have their biggest impact on delivery of the strategy, particularly if the staff development structure can also pull in the practical assistance of other champions and enthusiasts within the organisation. Many services prefer to use E-Guides for one to one support in actual classroom situations or on a referral basis. Few staff is willing to make a leap of faith in changing practice. They do not want to put the learners' experience and outcomes at risk. Nor do they want to take the chance of it all going wrong and feeling personally exposed or foolish.

This is one reason why the use of E-Guides in a one to one support role, both in the development of learning opportunities and subsequently in the classroom is so effective, even if it seems to be an expensive use of time when compared to large group training sessions. It is the impact on practice that is important and by supporting individuals closely E-Guides can ensure that tutors have the confidence to take the first step.

The key people to focus on in this equation are the individual teachers and their needs. In terms of effectiveness in our context of delivering the strategy, the value of the E-Guides must ultimately be assessed on whether the individual practice changes, as measured by teaching observation, learner feedback and appraisal. The only real way to achieve this is likely to be one to one interventions in the first instance, supplemented where possible by the contribution of enthusiasts within the staff team, whether formally or informally.

A successful e-mentoring scheme introduced by Derby Adult Learning Service pairs an experienced tutor who is confident in using technology with a less experienced colleague. The mentor provides support on a one-to-one basis, while those who are mentored supplement this by working together in peer groups. A measure of success has been that some of those supported by the programme in its early stages have now themselves become mentors.

The key concept is that of enabling staff to develop: to train them, to support them right through into the classroom or learning situation and to make sure that once they are there they have the necessary equipment. This last is a problem for managers to address.

Suffolk County Council ACL employed three dedicated E-Guides to visit courses across all curriculum areas and to sites scattered around the county. They were successful in raising awareness and skills levels, delivering some well received training, but noted that:

> One of the main issues that occurred for staff was the lack of access to technology in their area.

If staff does not have access to equipment in the classroom or learning situation all of the training effort and support is wasted.

Support for learners

The prime purpose of deploying technology within a learning provider's programme is to enhance the quality of learning experiences for each learner. Adult learners will arrive with great differences in both their skills level in using technology and in their readiness to use technology for learning.

There may be dramatic variations in:

- learners' motivation to use technology as part of their learning

- learners' level in use of technology

- learners' level of access to equipment away from the learning centre.

Front line teaching staff will have primary responsibility for taking account of these variations and managing the learning group to ensure that all learners have equality of access. However staff must be backed up with organisational level support.

It can be helpful if a provider includes a statement about access to use of technology within their learner charter or 'learner entitlement'. This could indicate that e-learning will be made available to enhance a course but that prior skills and knowledge or equipment will not be required. It is also good practice to include learners in the organisation's strategic development process and curriculum planning. In this way, learners can have a direct impact on learning provision.

Example of possible component of learner entitlement

> *When you join a learning programme with us, your teacher will offer a range of learning methods and this may include e-learning in the classroom or access to online activities and materials between classes. These e-learning elements will enrich the mix of learning activities available to you. However, you will not need any previous knowledge of e-learning to undertake the course and you will not normally require any additional specialist equipment.*

By including, within an initial assessment of learners, information on current information and communications technology (ICT) skill level, it is possible to identify immediate needs for skill training and support, and to track patterns of need. Following assessment, learning providers can then offer signposting to targeted resources such as the BBC Webwise website (see Further information p.48) or locally created 'help sheets'. Information for learners can also signpost places which provide out of class technology access such as UK online centres and public libraries.

Infrastructure: Get it used

The final step towards enabling staff enablement to bring about change in practice is providing appropriate infrastructure and sufficient equipment. The term infrastructure refers to the set of technical services that supports e-learning across the organisation. The most notable elements of teaching and learning infrastructure are:

- the stock of computers, digital and peripheral equipment that is available for teachers and learners to use, networked together on each site or location and connected to the internet as appropriate.

- communications facilities, such as email, social software (see 'Further information', p. 48)

- a learning platform.

In the short term, the main elements of infrastructure must be regarded as a fixed quantity, set out in the strategy and action plan to be purchased or otherwise obtained e.g. by negotiating access to a third party's equipment. The infrastructure of most education and training organisations is effectively fixed at the start of each academic year, if for no other reason than that teachers have sorted out their scheme of work and teaching plan for each course and are unwilling or unable to make radical change half way through just because more computers, better internet access or a new learning platform have become available.

A distinguishing features of adult learning compared to other sectors of education is the extent to which much of the infrastructure in use belongs to someone else – schools, colleges, libraries, third-party contracted providers. Therefore it is often subject to restrictions such as lack of easy access: locked doors, a lack of technical support and the requirements of another organisation's policies, procedure and rules.

Government funding channelled through NIACE has been the key to investment in kit, software, content and services. Many, though not all sites and venues, have Internet connectivity, whether it be broadband access through the JANET network or some other arrangement. The dispersed nature of ACL and the huge number of sites served, has led some enthusiastic tutors to improvise simulations of Internet connectivity where it does not exist. For example, they have placed Moodle or web pages onto laptops to mimic the functionality of a learning platform or web access. This imaginative commitment to getting the most out of available resources should be encouraged and supported.

There is no correct infrastructure that all Services must have or aim for. This is good news because the complexities listed above suggest it would be pure serendipity to pull an ideal solution together across the many sites and providers that make up provision.

This disparity and the difficulty of achieving an ideal planned infrastructure constrain and shape the e-learning strategy and action plan. At a practical level, however, the important issue becomes **maximising the use of what you have already got.**

In terms of enabling and encouraging change in teaching and learning practice it is important that teachers have as much access to equipment as possible, both for refining and developing their skills outside the classroom and for use with learners.

The main areas to address are:

- negotiating and policing levels of access to kit in contracted infrastructure

- ensuring that (portable) kit moves to where it is needed most

- measuring and monitoring equipment use. Despite the general inappropriateness of targets, it is important to ensure that equipment gets used, not least because its active life is often ended by technological advance making it obsolete rather than wear and tear making in unusable.

Maximise the use of existing stock

Surveys of equipment use throughout education typically reveal very low utilisation rates. These can be as low as 25 per cent, that is, equipment spends three hours out of every four unused. Increasing the rate of use has the same effect as getting more equipment – at a much lower cost, even if there is additional wear and tear. This can be achieved by making classrooms into open-access areas, having portable rather than fixed machines and introducing a loan scheme for tutors (or learners).

Cambridgeshire County Council provides a good example of this. An audit of equipment held in the Council was compiled and circulated to the Adult Learning Staff Group to collect further information. A schedule of the equipment held at the main site was set up and a method for borrowing equipment established.

Guidance on how to use the equipment was written, together with practical demonstration sessions. These sessions, showing how to use equipment and suggesting good practice were taken around the Service's dispersed sites, including a number of small village colleges, at times when tutors were on site and available, that is, before or after their classes.

The result was a significant increase in the use of the equipment – in effect an increase in the teaching infrastructure brought about by actively seeking to get stuff used. This could be measured and managed, moreover, because the Service had an accurate and centrally administered register of equipment as a result of the audit. Many services struggle to pull together such a list because equipment and software has been acquired historically through individual departmental budgets and sits on shelves or in tutors' drawers as the personal property of the curriculum area.

This might seem superficially trivial, but the general principle of 'sweating the assets' – making them work as much as possible - is particularly important in the context of enabling staff to deliver change and ensuring that skills to which teachers are exposed in training carry through into teaching and learning.

An example:
Westminster Adult Education Service

The e-learning Co-ordinator for Westminster Adult Education, a dedicated post with senior management support, steered curriculum areas towards a significant change in teaching and learning practice, including:

- implementing a Virtual Learning Environment (VLE)

- providing training and ongoing support for staff

- ensuring that classrooms are adequately resourced.

When the Co-ordinator joined the service he found a strategy in place that was,
> *... half way developed before my arrival and from there I chose to put in an action plan.*

Scott instigated discussions with each of the curriculum areas, using the NLN Transformation Tool as a method of assessing each area's current position and future expectations and hence to set targets. Once the learning area managers knew where they were going they were responsible for disseminating this information to other members of their staff. It was not clear how well this was done across the board, but he had a set of agreed aspirations within each area to report to senior managers.

Delivering the Promise

The vision was communicated effectively to managers by requiring them to think about e-learning and then demonstrate their understanding by taking action – in this case to set goals for their area. This was aggregated into a strategy and an action plan that was then made freely available to anyone in the Service to see.

> We didn't fully push it as well as we could have in terms of that we didn't then send it out to all tutors saying 'please look at this'.

Instead the job of reinforcing the communication task fell to the specialist E-Guides, one for each of the six curriculum area. Each E-Guide worked with their respective area manager to produce and to help implement an action plan. This broadened the e-learning base, increasing staff skills and expertise in the areas. Direct involvement of the E-Guides in the process of action planning meant that they were fully aware and committed to the strategy.

With these foundations in place, a staff development programme was based on drop-in sessions for initial training of staff on existing equipment. Critical to success was ensuring that staff could put their training into practice by having access to appropriate equipment.

> I think a key factor here is infrastructure – we didn't have any infrastructure of any form apart from three interactive whiteboards that weren't being used when I took my role. We've since got the investment and we now have an interactive whiteboard in every single room and a computer. I think that's key – if you haven't got that then the staff is going to say how are we going to do that if we haven't got the equipment. Those things need to be in place otherwise it is useless giving out staff training if there's nothing to use.

Whilst refurbishment and improvement of infrastructure was under way, the Co-ordinator and colleagues introduced the Information Technology Qualification (ITQ) programme (see 'Further information', p. 48), which looks to develop information technology (IT) skills in the context of the sector – in this case for teaching, learning and curriculum practice.

The Service developed its own bespoke course unit and with government funding via NIACE was able to pilot assessments for staff, so that they now have sector-specific assessments for eight different units for ITQ.

Previous low attendances at training events increased dramatically as occasional voluntary generic IT skills workshops were replaced by scheduled weekly sessions offering qualification-linked programmes centred around curriculum development and teaching practice, which helped to meet the new

Institute for Learning (IFL) (see 'Further information', p. 48) requirement for continuing professional development.

A key initiative in changing practice has been the implementation of a VLE, Moodle.

We were well behind other instigators of Moodle but we immediately saw the potential and we got onto it straight away. We've made a few mistakes along the way but overall it has been very successful in terms of being a very stable environment and being able to deliver what the tutors need.

It was introduced into the IT suites allocated to basic skills and ESOL courses. Tutors were supported by staff who shadowed them in the classroom, giving them suggestions as to what could be achieved and showed them how to upload their resources for each weekly session onto the VLE.

Initially members of staff were asked to upload their own course information, scheme of work and learning resources into Moodle but it soon became clear that this was a barrier to steadily increasing use in the classroom environment. The central team undertook this work and went on to bulk-load a number of courses onto the VLE. This has been strikingly effective in enabling change in practice. New learners in the area are assigned to a named teacher who has access to all of the existing materials on the learning platform.

That's the key – it's never a backwards step – the resources are there for that level of work and the teacher who comes in can look up the resources, pick up the scheme of work, change it for their own use and then carry on. It's all part of our quality assurance systems to guarantee a minimum level and having a standard on the VLE for all courses and then for the teachers to personalise that for their classes.

In some curriculum areas, including IT, teaching practice has been changed completely:

They just turn up and teach now so they are teaching out of the VLE and the same within the Skills for Life and ESOL – they don't use the web at all – they just use the VLE. The students know that they can go there too and pick up resources whenever they want.

Around a quarter of Westminster's courses now have course documents and learning resources on Moodle, with development ongoing. The key to changing practice for Westminster has been the combination of regular training sessions, follow-up in class support and access to the VLE – a coherent staff enablement approach targeted firmly on delivering improvements in teaching and learning.

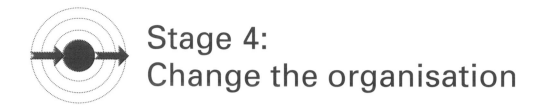

Stage 4:
Change the organisation

Changing the organisation

Few organisations in any sector of education would claim to have genuinely transformed themselves through the application of e-learning. A number, including some American universities, have developed substantial programmes of online learning, which are marketed globally, whilst many British higher education (HE) establishments combine web access with online materials to deliver courses overseas.

The University for Industry (Ufl) (see 'Further information', p. 50) has delivered courses under the learndirect brand to over 2 million learners since its inception in 2000. This is not the norm in post-16 education. Nor would we expect it to be the vision that is driving the e-learning strategy of adult learning or further education providers, let alone establishments in the voluntary sector, prisons and offender learning etc.

The 'Delivering the promise' model sets it sights somewhat lower than total transformation. Its final stage is to bring about a change in the organisation that will achieve and *sustain* the goal at the centre of the model: improving teaching and learning practice.

Some pragmatic actions to deliver this are:

- incorporating e-learning explicitly into the programme of teaching observation and performance appraisal

- accessing expertise and information from outside the organisation

- sustaining development and moving forward.

Teaching observation and performance appraisal

The observation of teaching is standard practice in education as part of the commitment to quality and to continuous improvement. Formal performance appraisal can be more problematical for an organisation with large numbers of sessional staff on short-hour contracts. Building the observation of e-learning practice explicitly into teaching observation brings together all of the assertions that have underpinned our model of change:

- it is focused on teaching and learning

- it monitors the extent to which management has been able to get staff to change practice

- it provides an opportunity to recognise and celebrate teachers doing their job well.

For all these reasons, teaching observation must both look for and record examples of e-learning. This fairly minor change at the level of the organisation is likely to have a dramatic effect on raising the profile of e-learning practice. It will lead to:

- staff and their line managers becoming aware that e-learning is recognised and valued by managers
- tutors planning e-learning activities explicitly into their schemes of work and lesson plans to enable observation to take place
- teaching observation staff becoming aware of the issues and opportunities and working with E-Guides
- E-Guides providing demand-led support that responds to requests from staff rather than pushing advice and guidance at them unasked.

It is hard to see how an organisation can deliver the promise of its e-learning strategy without incorporating e-learning into observation and appraisal of teaching and learning. The message to staff is clear: managers believe that e-learning is an important component of this organisation's work with learners and are committed to making it happen.

This brings us back to the starting point of Stage 2 of the model (Change the individual): the problem of communicating the vision and strategy for e-learning. We noted then that the best way to get staff to really come to grips with the strategy was to get them to do something in response to it.

Building e-learning into teaching observation will help to achieve this. There is a good case for not paying special attention to the use of technology, on the grounds that it is, after all, only another form of learning and the elements of good practice are essentially the same regardless of how you go about it: clarity of purpose, attention to individual needs, active involvement and engagement by learners, timely assessment of learning outcomes, etc.

Whilst this is true, it does not take into account what we are trying to do: to change practice and to deliver a strategy, which has been devised to improve learning and teaching. If we ask people to change, it is important to look for evidence of change and publicly recognise it. This will both reassure and reward staff for their effort.

There is an interesting contrast with the disappointment expressed by many staff when external inspections fail to make special notice of innovative practice.

Accessing expertise and information: working with others

Relying wholly upon your own resources for expertise, being content to learn by doing and to take your own mistakes on the chin is not always a recipe for success in delivering e-learning strategy. At best it will extend the timescale at each pioneering forward step. At worst it will incur unnecessary costs and be dogged by continual setbacks. There are two possible routes around at least some of these issues:

- working with partners
- working with experts.

Both also have the advantage of improving the prospect for sustaining development into the longer term.

Working with partners

Partnership working of one sort or another is a characteristic of the ACL sector, where much of the delivery is either through outsourcing to an independent provider or in contracted premises. If nothing else, this gives managers in the sector a less than starry-eyed insight into the business realities of partnership arrangements.

Working with partners is effective when it enables

- access to greater resources or expertise
- joining together to get the benefits of larger scale
- improved access to funding.

In smaller organisations and in areas such as the voluntary sector and offender learning partnership working may be the only practical way to address the use of technology for learning at any scale. It certainly has advantages in terms of bidding for public sector funds, including those available through European schemes.

We have already looked at Portsmouth's services in earlier examples. Portsmouth is a small unitary authority that has recognised the benefits of working with others locally, like Southampton, Isle of Wight and Hampshire County Council to generate successful joint bids for funding, including European Social Fund money. These have supplemented the funding

Portsmouth has won independently on the evidence of their strong strategic approach to e-learning and has been used to train and develop staff as well as to create and consolidate supporting posts in the service. The partners have benefited similarly.

Hartlepool is in partnership with other local authorities in the Tees Valley consortium, which has the responsibility to provide a virtual learning environment to all local authority learners in the Tees Valley, estimated to be around 30,000. Effective partnerships with the five members of the Tees Valley consortium have helped the development of online resources. Inputs from the Regional Support Centre – Northern – and the local Learning and Skills Council have also had a positive effect on the development of learning platform.

Using the experts

Government-funded support typically divide into two components:

1. A local or institution-based approach, which makes funding or targeted resource available free or at a subsidised rate for each establishment, or through bidding for project monies.

2. A national or regional approach, which sets up or supports a wider resource. This is usually managed through existing agencies, such as NIACE, Becta and the Joint Information Systems Committee (JISC), who are paid for delivering particular initiatives or outcomes.

In the context of e-learning, the work of these agencies has included nationwide services such as the free JANET broadband connection, the NLN multimedia learning materials and the E-Guides programme (see Further information p. 48). The lead agency for each sector is usually charged with managing specific projects, which has seen NIACE charged with oversight of funding opportunities such as capital grants, the learning platforms programme and the e-learning consultancy scheme.

There is an element of serendipity in how some of these projects turn out. At least part of the justification for funding projects, which take organisations into new territory, is that it helps them to bear the risks of unknown outcomes and potential failures.

Despite running highly professional awareness campaigns to promote their programmes, the agencies recognise that use of the national services is patchy. Some organisations make extensive use of the websites, seminars, conferences, advisory and guidance services provided by the national agencies and regularly bid for project funding. Others are either unaware or indifferent.

One influential factor in this is whether the service has a dedicated e-learning manager, or a manager for whom it is a substantive part of the role. Keeping track of national schemes and opportunities and taking advantage of them must be a central part of that role. The agencies look to use E-Guides as named contacts within an organisation, who might therefore be expected to learn about and flag up the potential not only of funding sources, but of all the free and subsidised resources available to support the implementation of e-learning.

Making effective use of this funded expertise is not only time-saving and cost effective; it is arguably an essential determinant of the ease with which a Service is able to achieve its e-learning goals.

JISC Regional Support Centres (RSC)

The Learning and Skills Council's e-learning programme set up and continues to fund nine regional centres of support, advice and guidance on aspects of e-learning managed through the Joint Information Systems Committee (JISC). These should be the first port of call for any Adult Learning Service.

The Regional Support Centre (RSC) employs a dedicated 'ACL advisor' many of whom should already be well known to staff, including the E-Guides in your Service. Each of the RSCs runs cost-effective training and awareness events and facilitates themed discussion forums for specialist groups, including technical, resource centre and curriculum staff.

Not only do the RSCs provide free advice, subject to reasonable requests and demands upon their time, they are often willing to sit on Steering Groups and committees. They are also well placed to act as a marriage broker for regional partnerships.

The City of York Adult and Community Learning Service worked with an RSC Advisor at the local RSC and a Moodle User Group to obtain both support and face-to-face training when implementing its learning platform. The same RSC acted as lead partner in a project involving Leeds Adult and Community Learning Service and its provider network of 27 separate organisations

RSC East Midlands set up an ACL E-learning Community for staff who has an e-learning remit. The group meets on a regular basis to share good practice and explore issues and has brokered a successful partnership bid for European funding to support the ongoing development of e-learning. Each of the RSCs has a similar track record.

At a national level they share information about effective practice, both in e-learning and in terms of their own successful intervention strategies, in order to work towards a consistent national standard of support with variations in response to local need. Despite their significance, high profile within the sector and promotional activities of the RSCs, many Services, for a variety of reasons do not take full advantage of them.

Hillingdon Adult Education, for example, was seriously delayed by technical problems with setting up Moodle before becoming aware that the RSC could help.

> *I am now more aware of the greater amount of help that is available...via JISC. I would not in future wait around for problems to be solved.., I would have asked for some external help.*
>
> Pat Gibbs, Hillingdon

Websites and other free materials

All of the main agencies have put together training and exemplar materials in recent years, many based upon free or commonly available software packages, including Microsoft Office. Some of these resources, now managed by the Learning and Skills Improvement Agency (LSIS) (see 'Further information', p. 48) have been in existence for over a decade and whilst some of the content is redundant, most continues to have value. There is a need to invest the time in search and discovery and to ensure that what is found can be flagged up and easily shared with staff who need the resource.

In addition to this general material there is a range of subject specific material available, either free on the web or in the form of specially developed packages, such as the NLN multimedia materials. The RSCs have staff who can advise on the best way to access this material and point to examples of good use and effective practice elsewhere.

The issue for each Service is to ensure that no matter who captures this information, it is disseminated to everyone who needs to know about it. The initial conduit for this might be E-Guides, but the strategic imperative to change the organisation is best served by moving towards making staff aware of resources and sharing them as a matter of course through established communities of practice. This is a development for which a learning platform is the only effective tool.

Working together

Electronic communications

A measurable indicator of organisational change is to be found in the reliance on electronic media, such as email and bulletin boards rather than hard copy documents as the everyday method of communication. If staff goes first to their email rather than their pigeon-hole, check the bulletin board rather than a notice board for news and search for policies and procedural documents on the intranet rather than in a filing cabinet then the organisation has truly begun to change. This is true even if the lack of a comprehensive network across all sites and all locations means that a back up system for some paper-based messages has to be maintained for the foreseeable future.

It is a telling indicator of commitment to technology and helps embed it into the commonplace daily routine. Where access to electronic communications for staff is impossible or difficult, as in prison education for example, its importance is particularly evident. A series of interviews with all of the providers of offender education in England recently found universal support for the notion that until the use of electronic communications became part of daily practice for teachers and learners it would be difficult to embed learning technology into teaching and learning practice.

Communities of practice

The final aspect of change in the organisation that we shall look at is the notion of communities of practice, or more accurately, communities of *practitioners*. Just as few organisations can field the necessary expertise and resource to get very far without the support of others, so too do individual practitioners struggle to find the time to discover, adapt and adopt the learning materials and good practice that they need.

Increasingly the professional associations who performed this role in the world of hard copy resources are shifting material onto the web. Even more important in the longer term is the spread of so-called social networking sites which provide interest groups with a forum to exchange news and views, together with a place to store and share resources. This can be done internally through the learning platform, with shared spaces for curriculum groups.

Services such as Cornwall Adult and Community Learning have a large numbers of tutors working in widely dispersed sites in scarcely populated areas. It uses its learning platform as a meeting place and swap shop for tutors who may never meet face to face from one year to the next.

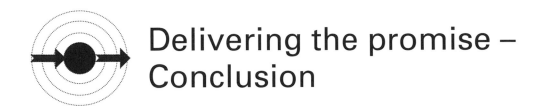

Delivering the promise – Conclusion

Delivering e-learning strategy in practice

The preceding sections have suggested a number of steps that can be taken to ensure that you deliver the promise of your e-learning strategy. If, as a leader with a serious intent to bring your vision to life, you have gone through the various stages and realised that you cannot commit the necessary resources, it might be timely to revisit and rethink your vision and strategy. You will need to bring your aspirations in line with what you are willing to resource. Use his checklist to remind yourself of the issues we have examined.

A checklist of factors for success in delivering e-learning strategy	
A dedicated manager for o lcarning	Or a significant part of another post
Senior management buy in	Leadership from the top
Engaging the wider organisation	Commitment of stakeholders
A review and self-assessment Process	Use the eLPS self-review tool, or an equivalent
A structure for staff development	Budget, Framework for individual support
E-Guides	Expertise and action on staff development needs and solutions
Communicating the vision	Active staff engagement not passive listening
A programme of staff training	Training opportunities Budget, pay for staff time
A programme of staff enablement	Time and resources to develop skills
A learning platform	A single place at the heart of e-learning A plan for getting it used Online training for staff

Infrastructure:	Maximise the use of existing stock Measure and monitor equipment use
Changing teaching practice	Enable change – time, access to equipment Support in the learning situation
Teaching observation and performance appraisal	Reward, recognition, reassurance
Working with partners	Peer organisations and professionals
Using the experts	RSCs Government and other funded agencies and organisations
Electronic communications	A comprehensive electronic information system
Communities of practice	Sharing resources Common documents

The basic four-stage model is a simplification of reality, but it is nonetheless a helpful guide to the processes and activities that are required to deliver e-learning strategy. The model is sufficiently generic to lend itself not only to other sectors but also, with suitable amendment, to other strategic challenges which require the same level of whole organisation planning, commitment and co-ordination.

It has been used as a framework on which to hang a number of key actions that the experience of e-learning development in ACL and elsewhere in education suggests will make a critical difference to success.

In working through the model we have called upon three unarguable assertions:

1. The purpose of educational establishments is to deliver learning.

2. Management is about getting other people to do things.

3. Teachers want to do their job well.

Again, the evidence in every sector seems to suggest that keeping these fundamental truths in mind when considering alternative options and making decisions is likely to lead to success.

The model sets out a roadmap for you as a leader to explore and exploit. Each of the factors for success justifies a publication of its own to bring out all of the complexities, challenges and opportunities. These books already exist, as do other sources of advice, guidance and expertise, including those we have already identified in the 'Further information' section of this publication.

The next step for you is to work through the model with staff and establish where there are gaps to fill and actions to take.

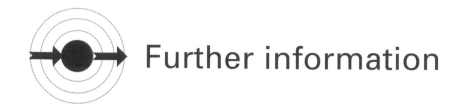

Further information

ACL eLPs (adult and community learning e-learning positioning statement)

The ACL eLPs (adult and community learning e-learning positioning statement) tool was an organisational self-review tool created by NIACE in collaboration with the then Centre for Excellence and the British Education and Communications Technology Agency (Becta). It has now been superseded by Becta's new self-review framework but is still available for use
http://matrix.becta.org.uk

British Broadcasting Corporation's (BBC) WebWise

WebWise is a short online course about the Internet designed for beginners and those who would like to improve their skills.
http://www.bbc.co.uk/webwise/

Becta Matrix

A collection of information technology and e-learning self-review tools for use by organisations and individuals.
http://matrix.becta.org.uk

E-Guides training

A national programme that aims to drive improvement in teaching by developing the e-learning skills and knowledge of 'E-Guides' to support colleagues in their use of technology.
http://www.niace.org.uk/Conferences/TrainingCourses/eguides.htm

ITQ (Information Technology Qualification)

The ITQ is the new Information Technology (IT) user qualification and training package that has been created by employers for employers to ensure that staff is trained in exactly the IT skills that they need to carry out their job roles.
http://www.niace.org.uk/information/Briefing_sheets/71-Using-ITQ.pdf

Institute for Learning (IfL)

Institute for Learning (IfL) is the professional body for teachers, trainers, tutors and student teachers in the learning and skills sector.
http://www.ifl.ac.uk/services/

JANET broadband connectivity and services

JANET is the network dedicated to the needs of education and research in the UK. The JANET network connects UK universities, FE Colleges, Research Councils, Specialist Colleges and Adult and Community Learning providers.
http://www.ja.net/

The Learning and Skills Improvement Service (LSIS) resources site

The Learning and Skills Improvement Service is the new sector owned body to develop excellent and sustainable FE provision across the sector. Its Excellence Gateway website provides practical help and resources for those working in the further education and skills sector.
http://teachingandlearning.qia.org.uk/teachingandlearning

Learning platforms and virtual learning environments (VLEs)

Learning platforms and virtual learning environments allow digital learning resources and activities to be accessed from a single online location. Moodle is one example of a learning platform (see below).
http://www.niace.org.uk/publications/P/Platforms.asp

Moodle learning platform

The website for all information related to the Moodle learning platform. Moodle is a system that can deliver and track learning.
http://www.moodle.com

NIACE e-Guidelines

A series of publications that provide guidance and support, accessible advice and useful examples of good practice for adult learning practitioners wishing to use digital technology in all its forms to attract and support adult learners.
http://www.niace.org.uk/Publications/E/E-LearningOutreach.asp#E-guides

NLN materials

A range of self-contained, multimedia rich digital resources covering a variety of curriculum areas and topics.
http://www.nln.ac.uk/

NLN Transformation Tool

A self review tool aimed at further education colleges and organisations.
http://excellence.qia.org.uk/page.aspx?o=ferl.aclearn.resource.id6415

Post-16 exemplars

A collection of examples of practice in the management and implementation of e-learning based on the experiences of adult learning and offender learning and skills providers.
http://www.niace.org.uk/exemplars/

Social software

Social software, such as blogs, wikis and bookmark sharing services, are tools that offer new ways for individuals to communicate and collaborate online.
http://www.jiscinfonet.ac.uk/infokits/social-software

Staff development e-learning centre (SDELC) website

A site aimed at providing a range of resources for practitioners and managers in the community based adult learning sector. The resources have been developed as self-study modules and are not facilitated. You need to register to use the site but registration is free.

http://www.sdelc.co.uk

University for Industry's (Ufi) learndirect

learndirect is a nationally recognised brand for learning and is a major supplier of learning delivered through the use of new technologies. It operates a network of more than 800 online learning centres in England and Wales.

http://www.learndirect.co.uk/